Original title:
Tropical Tranquility

Copyright © 2025 Creative Arts Management OÜ
All rights reserved.

Author: Dean Whitmore
ISBN HARDBACK: 978-1-80581-539-6
ISBN PAPERBACK: 978-1-80581-066-7
ISBN EBOOK: 978-1-80581-539-6

The Art of Resting in the Shade

In the hammock sways so light,
A cat spins dreams in my sight.
Ice cream drips down my chin,
  As the sun declares its win.

Lemonade in fluffy clouds,
I'm lost among cozy crowds.
Birds gossip in leafy trees,
Who needs to move with such ease?

Fronds Dancing in Gentle Wind

Palm leaves swing, a leafy ballet,
While I sip my drink and sway.
A lizard makes a sunbaked dash,
To join in on this beachy flash.

Tropical breezes steal my hat,
I chase it down like a goofy cat.
Waves giggle on the sandy shore,
I trip and splash, oh, to explore!

Solitary Moments Beneath the Banyan

Under roots that twist and twine,
I ponder if my snack's divine.
A squirrel glares, a nut in hand,
As if to say, "It's my command!"

The air is warm with silly cheer,
I smile as frogs croak loud and clear.
Each shade a chance to close my eyes,
To make sense of all the skies.

A Canvas of Colors in Still Waters

In the pond, ducks paint their tales,
Splashes seem like whimsical gales.
I toss a pebble, it plops and jumps,
As frogs join in, making grumpy thumps.

Reflections shimmer, oh so bright,
While fish plot disco in the light.
Nature's canvas, splattered hues,
A giggle here, a splash of blue!

Morning Mist and Marshmallow Clouds

The sun peeks in, a sleepy eye,
While morning fog begins to sigh.
A bird in pajamas takes to flight,
Chasing shadows, a comical sight.

Coffee brews like a wise old sage,
While squirrels dance, a fuzzy page.
The mist wears hats of fluffy fluff,
Even the breeze says, 'That's enough!'

Palm trees giggle, swaying light,
They whisper jokes that feel just right.
Sand crabs chuckle in tiny suits,
Dancing to tunes of funky roots.

As the day awakens, smiles spread,
On marshmallow clouds, no worry or dread.
With laughter echoing through the scene,
Who knew paradise could be so keen?

A Canvas of Coral Calm

Coral reefs in wild, bright hues,
Where fish wear shoes and share the news.
A parrotfish plays a ukulele tune,
Under a sky of a bubblegum moon.

Jellyfish float, all soft and round,
In a jelly ballet, they jump and bound.
Sea turtles wearing shades of cool,
Join the party, it's a splashy pool!

The starfish pose, all ten on deck,
Practicing moves, oh what the heck!
With crabs that tap dance on the floor,
This ocean giggle leaves us wanting more.

And when the tide whispers its final fare,
We'll salute the joy and the silly flare.
Here in the waves, we find our balm,
Who knew the sea could be so calm?

Lakes of Lapis Lazuli

Under the sun, lakes shimmer bright,
With turtles in shades of turquoise delight.
Frogs play leapfrog, just for a tease,
While fish gossip with a gentle breeze.

Picnics hosted by ants with flair,
They serve up crumbs, quite the affair.
A family of ducks dons tiny hats,
Strutting in style, even with chitchats.

The water mirrors the laughter above,
Where every ripple feels like love.
Mice in boats, paddling with cheer,
As the wind joins in, it's music we hear.

With sunset painting the skies so bold,
Every moment shared is a treasure to hold.
In lakes of blue where dreams unfurl,
It's a silly dance in a wacky swirl.

Whispering Waves

Waves are giggling, what a sight,
Tickling the sand with pure delight.
Seagulls crack jokes, a salty crew,
While crabs on the shore join in too.

Beach balls bounce with a playful glee,
Knocking over sunscreen, oh whee!
Kids build castles with moats of sand,
Where mermaids take a vacation, unplanned.

The sun's a comedian, wearing shades,
Making shadows dance in funny parades.
As laughter floats on the salty air,
We join the waves, without a care.

With stars twinkling over the sea,
The night is alive with glee and spree.
In the whispers of waves, joy weaves,
As we dance under skies that never leave.

Reclining in Radiance

In a hammock swaying wide,
I found a parrot as my guide.
He squawked a joke, oh what a tease,
While I sipped from a coconut breeze.

The sun chuckled, burning bright,
As I tried to nap, but what a sight!
A lizard danced on my left foot,
And I couldn't help but laugh, who knew it could be cute?

Palm trees wiggle to the beat,
While crabs scuttle across my feet.
Each splash from the ocean's sway,
Tickled my toes throughout the day.

As I dozed, a monkey swung,
Made a face and then just hung.
With laughter echoing all around,
Who knew relaxation could be so sound?

Serenity Among the Shadows

In the shade of a mango tree,
I found a nap, who could believe?
A squirrel stole my snack with flair,
I chased him off with a floppy stare.

The breeze giggled through the leaves,
As I kicked back, my heart believes.
A sleepy iguana yawned so wide,
His dreams of salad, fun to bide.

Coconuts plopped from branches high,
A gentle thump, oh my oh my!
Each time I jumped, I'd crack a grin,
Nature's comedy show, where to begin?

With laughter bubbling like the sea,
I dawdled blissfully, carefree.
Among the shadows, joy does dwell,
In these playful moments, all is well.

Lost in the Lushness

In verdant jungles, I lost my hat,
A monkey grabbed it—imagine that!
He wore it proud, a king of play,
While I joined in on this wild ballet.

Vines tangled round my legs, oh dear,
A snake slid by with a cheeky sneer.
"Just hang loose!" he seemed to say,
As I tripped over ferns in a silly way.

Colorful birds, they squawked and flew,
While I practiced yoga, feeling blue.
A goat strutted by, oh what a sight,
Winking at me, making everything right.

Laughter echoed amidst the leaves,
As the sun dipped low, and light deceives.
In this lush land, with joy I twirl,
Lost in hilarity, what a whirl!

Ocean's Harmonious Embrace

Waves giggle as they kiss the shore,
Seagulls squawk while they ask for more.
Sandy toes in the sun's warm glow,
Shells whisper secrets, but they move slow.

Starfish dance with clumsy grace,
Crabs do the cha-cha, keeping pace.
An octopus steals a beach ball tight,
As we all laugh at this silly sight.

Lush Escape

Palms sway like they're hula dancing,
Monkeys swing, while the birds are prancing.
Smoothies spill beneath the sun,
Fruits say, 'Hey, let's have some fun!'

Coconuts play peek-a-boo on trees,
As tourists nap, the sun's a tease.
Frogs croak jokes in a leafy hide,
While lizards strut, full of pride.

Gentle Waves and Gilded Sands

The sun's a lazy cat in the sky,
As I float like a potato, oh my!
Kids build castles that soon will crash,
While the wind plays tunes with a splash.

A beach ball rolls with a giggly shove,
While sunscreen fights like a wrestling glove.
Flip-flops flurry in a hasty race,
As laughter fills this sunny place.

Island Dreams

The hammock's swaying to a silly beat,
As I try to nap, but can't find my seat.
Cocktails bob in a dance, so spry,
While pineapples wink, oh my, oh my!

A turtle takes selfies, just for fun,
While a dolphin photobombs in the sun.
With laughter echoing across the bay,
Life here feels like one big play.

Hibiscus Hues at Twilight

Hibiscus blush as day departs,
Laughing flowers, nature's arts.
They giggle in the dusky light,
Whisper secrets, oh what a sight!

A parrot sneezes, what a fuss,
While palm trees sway without a rush.
The sun drips down like sticky honey,
Just another day, isn't it funny?

Fish swim by with silly grins,
Caught between the world of fins.
Stars peek through the fiery haze,
"What's with this twilight?" they seem to say.

The Calm Embrace of Island Skies

Clouds wear flip-flops, what a scene,
Drifting slow, so sweet and green.
A coconut falls, but don't you fret,
It just wanted to surf, I bet!

Waves giggle as they kiss the shore,
Tickling toes, then laughing more.
Seagulls squawk in a funny dance,
"Come join us, it's a beach romance!"

Sunset paints with vibrant cheer,
While fireflies join, ever near.
In skies that cradle, soft and bright,
Nature chuckles at our delight.

Swaying Shadows in the Midday Sun

Lizards in sunglasses, so cool,
Basking on the golden pool.
Shadows sway like they're in a jig,
As the sun hangs large and big.

Coconuts shake like maracas play,
Saying, "Let's dance! What's your say?"
Palm fronds clap, a rowdy crew,
They wave hello and bid adieu.

The heat's a blanket, thick and warm,
Yet here we laugh, we dodge the swarm.
"Why is that tree wearing a tie?"
Flip-flops slap as we wander by.

A Retreat in the Canopy

Up in the trees, the monkeys chatter,
Swinging around, what's the matter?
"Hey, pass the bananas, will ya, mate?"
Nature's jesters, feeling great!

Leaves rustle with a sneaky giggle,
While snails race, but oh so little.
Moths spin tales of nighttime fun,
While crickets beat, the beat goes on.

A hammock sways, 'neath the stars bright,
Rocking gently, oh what a sight!
As laughter echoes through the night's veil,
The jungle sings a merry tale.

Mornings Wrapped in Vanilla Air

The sun peeks in, a cheeky grin,
Birds sip coffee, let the fun begin.
A cat in shades lounges on a chair,
Dreaming of fish in a vanilla air.

Pancakes stack up like a tower high,
Butterflies dance with a joyful sigh.
Coffee's brewing, oh what a race,
Even the toast wants a slice of space.

Sipping slow, the giggles flow,
The cereal swims in a milky glow.
A squirrel steals snacks just for fun,
Chasing the sun till the day is done.

Lush Green Secrets of Paradise

In the jungle, a parrot's joke,
Snakes whisper secrets that make them choke.
Lizards lounge with laid-back flair,
Wearing sunglasses, without a care.

The monkeys swing, their laughter loud,
Waving goodbye to the curious crowd.
In petals bright, a blushing bloom,
Invites a raccoon to join the room.

A frog jumps high, says, "Look at me!"
Finding his rhythm, a bouncy spree.
While turtles dream, oh what a sight,
In lush green peace, everything feels right.

The Rhythm of Rain on Leafy Canopies

Raindrops tap, a quirky beat,
Dancing on leaves, a soggy treat.
A hedgehog slips, makes quite the splash,
While frogs all clap with a croaky bash.

Umbrellas open, a colorful show,
Rainbow socks on feet below.
Clouds play tag in the gloomy sky,
As droplets spill, giggles amplify.

A puddle jumps with joy so true,
Reflecting smiles in a watery hue.
Nature hums with a playful cheer,
In every storm, there's fun to steer.

Embracing the Warmth of Distant Horizons

Far away lands whisper and hum,
A turtle dreams of a distant drum.
Waves chuckle softly, secrets to share,
As sunsets paint skies in a fiery flair.

Toucan taps, a wacky tune,
While shells spin stories beneath the moon.
Footprints dance on sandy shores,
A crab leads laughter while everyone roars.

The breeze tells tales of far-off lands,
Where fish wear hats and chefs have bands.
With warmth that tickles the joyful heart,
Adventure awaits where silliness starts.

Footprints in the Soft Sand

In the sand, we danced like ducks,
Chasing crabs with silly clucks.
Each footfall leaves a story bold,
Of beachside antics, giggles untold.

Seagulls squawk, they think they're neat,
Catching snacks, oh what a treat!
But none can rival our sliding grace,
As we trip and tumble, a comical race.

The sun's a jester, shining bright,
Melting ice cream in the light.
With sticky hands and happy grins,
We laugh as each new mishap begins.

So here's to fun, and sandy toes,
Where every jest and joy just grows.
We'll leave our footprints as we play,
In the sand, forever we'll sway.

The Silent Call of the Coast

At dawn, the waves whisper a tune,
Calling dolphins to dance by noon.
Shells giggle softly, lining the shore,
While seaweed wigs have us begging for more.

Beach balls bounce, then pop with flair,
As gulls swoop down, swoon in mid-air.
With sandy shirts and flip-flops askew,
We chase our dreams in a sea of blue.

The sun wears shades; it's quite a sight,
Catching sunburns and sun-kissed fright.
We lounge like lizards, on the hot, warm sand,
While the tide pulls in with a slippery hand.

Oh, coastal magic, quirky delight,
Where every splash adds joy to the sight.
Let's gather giggles and laughter sweet,
As the beach keeps calling, can't miss that beat!

A Lullaby of Lush Landscapes

In jungles thick, where monkeys play,
Bananas drop in a comical spray.
Parrots squawk with colors bright,
Watching us trip, what a sight!

With leafy hats and arms out wide,
We dance with vines, no need to hide.
The plants just giggle, swaying slow,
As we tumble through, putting on a show.

The breeze tickles, the palm fronds sway,
While bugs play hide and seek all day.
Each flower's face smiles up at me,
Joining the fun, oh what glee!

So let us roam through this vibrant maze,
In laughing joy, we'll spend our days.
With nature's laughter, wild and free,
A lullaby sung, just you and me.

Where the Ocean Meets the Sky

The horizon plays tricks, oh so sly,
Where water winks at the bluest sky.
Waves wave back with a splash and a grin,
Teasing flip-flops and our giggly kin.

Surfboards wobble like baby deer,
As we surf through foam without a fear.
Each tumble makes a splashy sound,
With laughter echoing all around.

Kite-flying squirrels spin with delight,
Chasing clouds in the soft, warm light.
Ocean and sky, a funny affair,
Nudging each other, as if to dare.

So grab your friends, let's make a scene,
As we chase sunsets, gold and green.
With carefree giggles, let's say goodbye,
To the silly dance where ocean meets sky.

Curled Up with the Coast

On the warm sand, a crab plays hide,
With a tiny fedora, feeling quite spry.
The seagulls squawk tales of a sandwich fly,
While sunscreen's the scent of a summer tide.

Pinch me, I'm dreaming, I must be a shill,
For the waves offer laughter, like a friendly thrill.
Flip-flops are dancing, they have such a will,
Oh look, there's a dolphin! Wait, was that a quill?

Palm trees are swaying like they're at a ball,
An iguana's the DJ, just having a crawl.
Marmalade sunsets, they put on a sprawl,
In this sunny playground, we all stand tall.

So here's to the coast, let's laugh and we'll sway,
With silly sun hats and cocktails on trays.
The beach is our circus, come join in the play,
Forever we'll cherish these whimsical days.

Echoes of Easy Living

Underneath the shade of a big banana,
Monkeys are plotting a game with a piano.
Tiki torches wink, say 'come join the fauna',
While cocktails are swirling in a green guana.

Lizards in sunglasses recline on the deck,
Swapping silly stories of their last trek.
Pineapples giggle, they're quite the fine speck,
In this land of easy, there's nary a wreck.

If only the clouds could share in this fun,
They'd form into shapes, oh, what's that? A bun!
With rainbows for ribbons, and laughter to run,
Every moment here feels like a sweet pun.

So raise up your glasses, with juice that does zing,
Let's toast to the ease that each day will bring.
In this land of delight, let's dance and we'll swing,
Where living is easy, like birds on the wing.

The Pulse of Paradise

A parrot is gossiping, oh what a tease,
While sandals revolt, abandon the tease.
Under coconut trees, everything's a breeze,
And the laughter from sunbathers puts minds at ease.

The waves write love letters on bright sandy shores,
Each splash tells a joke, oh, but wait, there's more!
A crab wearing shades struts just like a chore,
While flip-flops join in, dancing on the floor.

Fruity drinks wave like they're at a parade,
An octopus joins in, but the blender's afraid.
Every sunset's a canvas, with colors displayed,
This pulse of pure fun, makes memories unmade.

From beach chairs we chuckle, with snacks piled high,
In this party of life, there's no time to sigh.
So come share the laughter, just give it a try,
Let's pulse with the paradise, as seagulls fly by.

Memoirs of Mellow Days

Floating on hammocks, like clouds gone away,
The sun's got a smile, it's brightening the day.
Pineapples waltz—what a curious display,
While the wind plays the ukulele's soft sway.

A turtle in shades takes his sweet, gentle time,
While birds overhead mimic jazz in their rhyme.
There's giggles and tickles as beaches align,
In this mellow mosaic, all is simply sublime.

Coconut water mixed with a splash of lime,
Makes sipping a pleasure, feels more like a crime.
The breeze tells the secrets, with rhythms so prime,
Entrancing the moment, as we drift and climb.

So here's to the memories of laziness grand,
With laughter and joy, like grains of soft sand.
In the diary of bliss, we'll write our own brand,
Of mellow days living, in this carefree land.

Emerald Canopies

Under leaves so green, we play,
Joking with the breeze all day.
Lively squirrels steal our snacks,
Waving branches laugh at our quacks.

Sunshine tickles, birds take flight,
Dancing shadows, a comical sight.
In this jungle, fun is free,
Even the monkeys chuckle with glee.

Waterfalls giggle as they flow,
Slipping rocks down below.
A misplaced splash on my face,
Turns my frown into a chase.

Emerald wonders, what a tease,
Swinging in hammocks, catching bees.
Here, the laughter reigns supreme,
Chasing joy is all our dream.

A Symphony of Stillness

In the calm where palm trees sway,
Even crickets learn to play.
A frog croaks a silly tune,
While fireflies dance by the moon.

Coconuts laugh as they drop,
Bouncing around, they never stop.
The air is thick with playful glee,
As waves crash down quite carelessly.

Sunbathers toss a frisbee wide,
Only to have it hit the tide.
Splashing water all around,
Joy is where the fun is found.

Stillness reigns, but not for long,
Nature hums its playful song.
Laughter echoes through the trees,
In this moment, all feels at ease.

Calm Between the Tides

Waves whisper tales of sandy dreams,
Where laughter flows in playful streams.
Footprints dance on soft, warm land,
While seagulls tease with mischief planned.

Shells collect secrets on the shore,
Each telling jokes from days of yore.
With buckets full of silly finds,
The ocean smiles, leaving us kind.

A beach ball bounces high and low,
Chasing kids all to and fro.
Splashing neighbors, whoops and cheers,
The sound of laughter fills our ears.

Here, serenity meets delight,
In every giggle, pure and bright.
Between the tides, we find our way,
With joy and jests, we choose to stay.

Serenity Under Coconut Trees

Coconuts grin with nutty grace,
While we lounge, at a slower pace.
The breeze shares tales of days gone by,
Under the sun, we laugh and sigh.

Palm fronds wave like cheerful fans,
Welcoming us with open hands.
Whilst lizards perform their little tricks,
We roll in laughter, dodging licks.

A hammock sways, a cozy trap,
One wrong move, and it's a nap!
With fruit smoothies in our grasp,
We sip and smile, not one to gasp.

Underneath this leafy cover,
We find the joy in being together.
In each soft rustle, a chuckle flows,
As nature's laughter gently grows.

Palettes of Paradise

In the garden, a parrot sings,
With hues so bright, it wears no bling.
Swaying people in hula skirts,
Chasing coconuts, oh how it hurts!

A sunburned shark, with shades on tight,
Did the limbo under moonlight.
Sipping smoothies, dripping down
While locals jest, 'He looks like a clown!'

The palm trees dance, a silly sway,
Crabs on parade, hip-hop all day.
Seagulls steal fries, and then some cake,
A feast for them—what a big mistake!

In this land where laughter breezes,
Even the sunsets wear party pleases.
With colors leaking, skies toasted pink,
Unicorns wish for a drink, I think!

Lullabies from the Lagoon

Frogs croak tunes by the lily pads,
As dragonflies dance, oh what a fad!
The turtles clap, with tiny hands,
While ducks gossip about their plans.

A sleepy fish dreams of sushi rolls,
As owls drop by with loud hoots and ghouls.
The water shimmers, giggles pierce,
It's hard to sleep as nature's fierce!

A beach ball floats, but no one cares,
The hammock swings—let's play musical chairs!
The stars peek down, a winking crew,
While fireflies boogie—join in, you too!

In this lagoon, where grins abound,
Serenades echo soft and round.
Each lullaby ends in a chuckle,
Who knew bedtime could cause so much buckle?

Hibiscus Dreams

Red blooms dance on a breezy day,
They have a party, come join the fray!
With bumblebees buzzing the latest news,
And daisies giggling in flamboyant hues.

A lizard in shades, a beach bum king,
Could teach us all how to cha-cha swing.
With flip-flops flying, what a sight,
Even the sun seems to shine more bright!

The sand wishes it could take a swim,
But instead, it lets seagulls spin on a whim.
Coconut pirates, they steal the show,
In hibiscus dreams, let's dance with a glow!

Oh, what a mess we made today,
Flower confetti strewn on display.
So raise a toast with juice so grand,
To hibiscus dreams and a wild, fun land!

Solace by Starlight

Underneath the moon, a turtle struts,
Strumming shells, wearing sea urchin cuts.
A starfish yodels, what a surprise!
While crabs attempt to play the wise!

The ocean giggles, churning up foam,
A mermaid's lyrics can't find a home.
With fish in sequins, they dance and twirl,
In this evening ball, it's a finny whirl!

Glowworms gather to share the stage,
In gentle waves, they flaunt their age.
While seaweed sways, a quirky crew,
Who knew starlight could bring such goo?

So raise your voice under the night,
Where laughter's the spark, and joy takes flight.
With solace brewing against the tide,
Life's quirks and giggles swell side by side!

In the Shade of the Banyan

Underneath wide branches, we doze,
Sipping coconut drinks, striking silly poses.
The monkeys swing by, stealing our snacks,
While we giggle loudly, no worries or lacks.

The sun plays hide and seek, oh what a game,
Bees buzz about, trying to stake their claim.
Banyan leaves tickle us, like a prank by fate,
We fling them aside, cause we just can't wait!

A gecko sneaks up, with a head full of glitz,
Chasing a butterfly, oh what a flit!
We cheer him on, like he's in a race,
While a parrot squawks, joining the chase.

Finally, we nap, in the shade's embrace,
Dreaming of laughter, and that monkey's face.
With a smile on our lips, and sand on our toes,
In the shade of the banyan, life just flows.

Surrendering to Stillness

Laid on a hammock, swinging with glee,
A mosquito buzzed, then darted at me.
I danced and I swayed, keeping time with the breeze,
While palm trees laughed, saying, "Do what you please!"

The ocean whispers secrets, soft like a dream,
As crabs on the shore create their own team.
While seaweed does tango, looking quite snazzy,
I join in their fun, feeling all kinds of jazzy.

A turtle pokes out, with a grin that's a hoot,
Winking at fishes, like he starts to pull loot.
We joke about pace, irony and flair,
In this stillness, life's circus floats in the air.

As twilight arrives, and stars start to gleam,
A firefly winks, opening the dream.
I chuckle at nature, all busy and colorful,
When even a shell has its own fun, so wonderful!

Vanishing Footsteps

Along the sandy beach, I leave little tracks,
A crab scuttles by, like, "Whoa, how he acts!"
With each wave that crashes, my footprints dissolve,
The ocean giggles, saying, "Time to evolve!"

I chase after crabs, they're quick and they're sly,
"Hey, wait!" I yell, as they wave me goodbye.
Seagulls above play a symphony right,
While I do my best not to trip in fright.

The sun dips low, painting skies with delight,
I dance on the shore, oh what a sight!
Like a silly sea star, I twirl and I leap,
In the fading day, the world whispers, "Keep!"

As darkness arrives, the footprints then wave,
My silliness lingers, I'm still trying to save.
With the ocean's laughter, a promise to hear,
No footsteps lost here, just echoes of cheer.

Nurtured by Nature

The jungle hums softly, like a warm lullaby,
As I sip lemonade, beneath the clear sky.
A parrot looks down, with a wink and a squawk,
"Your drink's not too fancy, let's take a walk!"

We march through the ferns, doing our best strut,
With vines tickling legs, we both laugh and tut.
The monkeys swing by, trying to join,
Making faces that echo, "Hey, isn't this fun?"

In the garden of laughter, flowers start to tease,
"Don't step on my petals, I'm trying to please!"
Their colors swirl wildly, like a painter's delight,
Creating a scene that glows through the night.

With fireflies twinkling, we twirl under stars,
Life's a comedy, full of giggles and spar.
In nature's warm hug, we laugh and we play,
Nurtured by shenanigans, brightening the day.

Serene Shores of Solitude

The waves they dance, a goofy twirl,
The seagulls squawk, give life a whirl.
Sunburned toes in sandy chairs,
I sip my drink, without a care.

The palm trees lean, they're in on the joke,
They wave their arms, oh what a poke!
The sun's a glutton, melting slow,
A giant fried egg, just so you know.

I built a castle, it fell in a rush,
A friendly crab left me in a hush.
"Not my fault," he said, with a grin,
I blame the tide, for checks and wins.

As day drifts out on a colorful slide,
I chuckle aloud, enjoying the ride.
With friends like this, oh what a scene,
Life's just a beach, if you know what I mean.

A Breath of Ocean Air

An old beach chair whispers my name,
As I sit down, it groans with fame.
The breeze is cheeky, tousling my hair,
I laugh and call it a tangled affair.

A crab by my foot gives me a stare,
"I swear I'm not dancing, just chillin' in air!"
The fish splash about, having wild fun,
While I sip at my drink, oh, isn't life run?

I chase seagulls, just to say 'hi',
They mock my moves, but I still try.
The sky rolls its eyes, a vivid blue,
Nature's reminder that fun's never through.

As clouds float by in a fluffy parade,
A sunlit sparkle is the prize that's laid.
With laughter and joy, a lively song,
Breathe deep, my friend, where you belong.

Floating Away into Quietude

Drifting on water, a rubber duck,
With pirates in dreams, oh what luck!
The sun's a joker, hiding behind,
Flipping its rays, a playful bind.

I spotted a fish, wearing a hat,
Gave me a wink—how peculiar is that?
My raft, my throne, upon the sea,
"Crown me the king!" I shout with glee.

The waves are giggling, a bubbly cheer,
I float by dolphins who draw near.
They flip and twist, I feel so spry,
While I'm dodging waves with a clownish sigh.

Sunset arrives, in wardrobe divine,
The palette swirls like a sassy wine.
Quietude reigns, with laughter's embrace,
Float away, my friend, it's a comical place.

The Stillness of Sunset

The day's last laugh, as the sun peeks,
Crayons in the sky have lost their streaks.
With marshmallow clouds, they dance in line,
While I munch on chips and sip on wine.

The ocean whispers, as shadows grow bold,
A seagull yells, "Hey! Behold!"
"Stop stealing my fries!" I shout in jest,
He flips me off, and then he rests.

The sunset's brush, a canvas wide,
Beckons the night with a midnight ride.
With giggles and chuckles, stars take their place,
As the moon twirls on in a silvery race.

So here I sit, on this sandy dance floor,
With laughter echoed, from shore to shore.
The stillness of sunset, a cheeky friend,
A merry affair that never will end.

Beneath the Mango Shade

Under the mango tree, I sit,
A squirrel steals my snack, what a wit!
He dances around, full of glee,
While I plot my revenge with a cup of tea.

The sun beams down, too hot to bear,
I fan myself with an old flip-flop pair.
A parrot squawks, 'What's up with you?'
I shrug, my life's like a zoo, it's true!

Lizards sunbathe, skitter about,
I try to catch one, but they pout.
Mangoes fall like sweet summer rain,
Most hit my head; I'm now mango-brain!

Still, laughter rings through the vibrant air,
With every slip, it's a comedy affair.
Life's simply perfect, though slightly absurd,
In the shade where weirdness is the word!

Rhythms of the Reef

Under the waves, fish swirl and sway,
A crab joins in, he thinks he's ballet.
I try to dance, but I trip on a fin,
'Just keep swimming!' I shout, with a grin.

Corals chatter like gossiping friends,
As turtles glide by, with no need to pretend.
I wave to a seahorse, it flips me the tail,
Said, 'Try my moves; they never fail!'

Jellyfish float, looking so grand,
With their bobbing bodies, a sight quite unplanned.
But I'm just here for that sweet, salty breeze,
Laughing with fish as they flick their fins with ease.

Oh, ocean, with your giggles and quirks,
Who knew sea life was such fun work?
Each wave tells a tale, so wild and free,
In the reef, we're all comedy kings, you see!

Solitude in Paradise

I sit on the shore, feeling so fine,
With coconuts dropping, a natural wine.
Seagulls squawk, as if they've met me,
I start to wonder if they want my margarita, oh wee!

The hammock sways like my brain in a spin,
As I munch on some chips, what a life I'm in!
A crab steals a chip and scuttles away,
I chase him while laughing; come back, I say!

Sunshine so bright, it's a sassy glow,
Each sunburnt thought is a funny show.
Lazy lizards wink, like they know my plight,
Where's my beach towel? It vanished from sight!

Still, in this bliss, I chuckle and sigh,
With every goofy moment, I reach for the sky.
The ocean hums softly, with laughs pure and sweet,
In my paradise, every blunder's a treat!

The Color of Calm

In shades of blue, my thoughts drift away,
A pineapple hat? Oh, what a display!
The waves whisper secrets, I hear them hiss,
But am I the only one who thinks this is bliss?

Palm trees swaying with an elegant tease,
The breeze whispers jokes, just catch them, please.
I chuckle at shadows; they tumble and play,
It's a comedy show in nature's bouquet.

A duck waddles by, quacking a tune,
With a flair so grand, just like a cartoon.
I join in the laughter, though I'm not in the act,
For nature's got humor; that's a simple fact!

So, here's to the calm that brings a soft cheer,
With laughter and silliness, nothing to fear.
With colors so bright, let's paint the day wild,
In this joyful palette, life's a carefree child!

Where Time Melts Like Ice Cream on Hot Days

On a hot day, the clock takes a turn,
Every tick makes the ice cream churn.
The sun's a baker, up high in the sky,
While I sit beneath, letting the minutes fly.

Laughter bubbles like soda in the sun,
Chasing around, oh! This day is fun.
Who knew time could slide off so sweet,
Like melting treats on my sunburnt feet?

Watermelon smiles from vendors nearby,
Cooling off with a fruit slice and a sigh.
Embracing the silly, the joy of today,
In this sticky bliss, I'll simply stay.

So join me here in this sticky delight,
Where time's a tease, and giggles take flight.
With every drip and each laughter-lined dream,
We savor the fun as the world turns to cream.

Whispers of the Palm Breeze

The palms are gossiping, oh what a show,
Their leaves are rustling like it's a cabaret glow.
Each breeze that wanders tickles my toes,
While I try to dance, but my balance just goes!

A parrot sings jokes from high in the tree,
And I laugh at the claims that he's funnier than me.
With a flip, a flap, he shows off his flair,
I pretend I can fly, but I'm stuck in my chair.

The sand's a tickler, it giggles and shifts,
As I bury my worries and find some new gifts.
Shells have the best tales when alone on the shore,
About crabs who wear hats and dance like the lore.

So let's listen close to the palm tree's jest,
With whispers of laughter, this day is the best.
In the shade of the leaves, we're all careless and free,
Join the palm breeze chorus; it's silly as can be!

Serenity by the Shoreline

At the shoreline, I lay with a sandwich in hand,
While seagulls laugh like they own the whole land.
I toss them a crumb, they squawk like they're mad,
Guess I'll stick to my chips, and my snacks go unclad.

The waves play peek-a-boo, quiet but sly,
With every splash, I'm like, "Oh my!"
The surf's a comedian, making me squeal,
As it tickles my toes, what a fun surreal!

A kid builds a castle, quite proud of his feat,
But the ocean, oh no! Just decided to greet.
He shouts in despair, his dreams swept away,
As I hide my giggles, it's the ocean's play.

But by the shoreline, laughter reigns supreme,
With every wave dancing, we savor the dream.
In this sandy theatre, let's all take a seat,
And enjoy the fun as life's treats can't be beat!

Sunlit Haven

In this sunlit haven, laughter's aglow,
We dance with the shadows, putting on a show.
The sun's our spotlight, it shines ever bright,
While butterflies giggle, taking off in flight.

With ice-cold drinks and silly hats too,
We lounge on the grass, pretending we flew.
A squirrel gives side-eyes, judging our cheer,
But we just wave back and raise up a beer!

Flowers are gossiping, sharing some tea,
While I twist and shout with a quirky old tree.
The breeze carries whispers of fun near and far,
As we all join in, and groove like a star!

In this sunny retreat, where giggles don't cease,
We find a sweet joy, a moment of peace.
With laughter and friendship, this haven we claim,
In sunlit delight, we all share the same game!

The Rhythm of Relaxation

Palm trees sway, a dance in the breeze,
Lizards sunbathe, having their ease.
The hammock swings, it's quite the show,
As seagulls squawk, 'Hey, come join the flow!'

Sipping coconut with a straw so wide,
Dancing to tunes of the ocean's tide.
Flip-flops flop as I take a stroll,
Finding lost snacks is my main goal!

The sun dips low, golden and bright,
Even my towel is feeling just right.
The beach ball rolls with a bounce and cheer,
Oh, who knew lounging could involve such beer?

As the stars come out, the crickets sing,
Life's a party; I'm king of this thing.
Under the moon, I strike a pose,
For the selfie of one, where carefree flows!

Nature's Gentle Whisper

A parrot squawks, sounding off-key,
While monkeys swing, laughing with glee.
The breeze tells jokes as it rustles the leaves,
And oh! The chattering of silly bees.

A turtle plods in a race quite slow,
'Catch me if you can!'—What a charming show!
Sipping on juice that drips like rain,
Feeling like royalty, though the throne's a drain!

The sun showers me with a playful grin,
While ants march in line, plotting their win.
A crab sidesteps, wearing a shell so grand,
I think he's the mayor of beachy sand!

At night, fireflies dance, a twinkling fest,
As I kick back, forgetting the rest.
With laughter in waves, and joy in the air,
Nature's a comedian, I swear, I swear!

Song of the Sundrenched Sea

Waves crash in time with my belly's grumble,
A dolphin flips, making my heart tumble.
The sunscreen's thick, a gloppy delight,
Cuz without it, my skin's a future fright!

The crabs do the cha-cha on the sandy shore,
While I wiggle between snacks and a bit more.
Seashells sing songs of the ocean's past,
But I'm just here for the sun and the laugh blast!

A beach umbrella turns in the gusty breeze,
Where I'll sip my drink on my knees, with ease.
The sunburn talks of my overzealous rows,
But nobody cares about a tomato's woes!

As the sun sets down, me feeling quite merry,
A sunset selfie with a splash of cherry.
In the land of fun, my spirit's set free,
Life's little moments - sea, sun, and me!

Lost in Leisure

Caught in a nap beneath a tree,
Dreaming of fish that talk to me.
I dive for a snack, swim in my mind,
While waves giggle, oh isn't life kind?

When the urge to explore tries to beguile,
I grab a piña colada and lounge for a while.
A crab with a hat shimmies on by,
Did he just wink? Oh my, oh my!

Sandcastles rise, each grain with a chuckle,
A tiny moat formed to prevent any shuffle.
The tide waves hello, with a splash of foam,
As I lounge in my kingdom, I feel right at home.

As twilight dances in colors so bold,
I laugh at my toes, all sandy and cold.
The stars whisper secrets in the night air,
In this land of laughter, I've found my fair share!

Sunlit Dreams on Sandy Shores

On sandy beaches where seagulls play,
A crab does a jig, in its own quirky way.
The sun shines bright, casting shadows like ever,
While flip-flops dance, oh how clever!

Waves tickle toes, a splash and a cheer,
As sunscreen flies, oh dear, oh dear!
Beach balls are bouncing, rolling so free,
Everyone's laughing, what a sight to see!

Frisbees go soaring, not one stays in place,
Sand castles crumble, a sandy disgrace.
A seagull swoops down, just trying to snack,
While sunburns remind us we're pale on the back!

At sunset we gather, with drinks in hand tight,
The day ends with giggles, all rosy and bright.
In dreams we'll be surfing, with dolphins a'play,
Chasing the moonbeams, we'll dance all the way!

A Melody of Leaves and Laughter

In the forest green, where the monkeys swing,
All branches are rattling, the birds start to sing.
A squirrel in a hat, so snazzy and neat,
Tries to impress, but trips on its feet!

The breeze whispers secrets, tickles our skin,
While turtles pose, as if they might win.
A picnic spreads out, with snacks in a row,
But ants have a party, oh no, oh no!

Leaves whirl around, like confetti in flight,
Chasing each other, oh what a sight!
The flowers are giggling, they can't keep it in,
While two bees are arguing on who gets to win!

By evening we gather, to share silly tales,
With fireflies buzzing as night softly pales.
We sway to the music, till stars light the skies,
In laughter we linger, with joyful surprise!

Coral Reflections at Dawn

Morning breaks softly, with colors bestowed,
Fish throw some shade, while the sun starts to load.
A turtle in glasses, just chilling with flair,
Ponders the meaning of seaweed and air.

Jellyfish giggle, with sways oh so smooth,
While a crab in a tie gets ready to groove.
Bubble-blowers perfect their craft with a grin,
Creating soft clouds, let the fun times begin!

Seashells are chatting, with stories to share,
Each one a treasure, from deep down there.
A dolphin does flips, oh what a clown,
Under the waves, where laughter abounds.

As day opens wide, with sunrays that dance,
All sea creatures join in, given the chance.
Together we laugh, as horizons we seek,
In this watery world, joy spills from each peak!

Dancers of the Ocean's Edge

At the ocean's edge where the tides like to play,
Crabs put on shows, in their own cabaret.
Starfish take selfies, with smiles that just glow,
And dolphins do cartwheels, putting on quite a show!

Waves step in rhythm, a dance oh so grand,
While beachgoers clap, with toes in the sand.
An octopus twirls, with colors ablaze,
It juggles some shells, in the sun's warming rays.

Seagulls join in, with their squawking refrain,
All creatures unite, in this hilarious chain.
A flip-flop flies high, like an overflying kite,
And everyone laughs at the unexpected sight!

As the sun begins sinking, the dance floor still gleams,
With sprites of the sea, who've forgotten their dreams.
But laughter remains, under stars shining bright,
As we dance at the ocean's edge, deep into the night!

Whispers of the Coconut Grove

Coconuts dangling, high in the air,
Sipping on juice, without a care.
A monkey steals snacks, what a bold feat,
While I sit and squish my sunscreened feet.

Parrots chatter, gossip flies by,
"Did you see Fred? He tried to fly!"
The breeze carries laughter, tickles my nose,
As palm trees sway in comedic pose.

Serenity Under the Palms

Under the palms, where shadows play,
I wrestle my hat, it's gone astray!
A crab in a shell, trying to dance,
Can't stop giggling, it's quite the chance.

My drink's a cocktail, bright and tall,
But I spill a bit, oh what a fall!
The lizards laugh, they find it so grand,
While I swipe up my colorful sand.

Echoes of a Caribbean Breeze

Waves whisper secrets, in hues of blue,
They mock my attempts at surfing, it's true!
Flip-flops take flight, like they've got wings,
I dive for them, hear the ocean sing.

A crab scuttles past, "Race you to shore!"
I follow its path, but trip and implore,
The sun beats down, my towel a throne,
With coconut dreams, I lay there alone.

The Gentle Lapping of Waves

The waves prance softly, a rhythmic cheer,
While seagulls squawk, it's quite the frontier.
My floatie's deflated, what a sad scene,
I paddle in circles, feel like a queen!

Salty snacks scattered, a feast for the ants,
They're having a party, and I must dance!
Laughter erupts, as sand sticks to skin,
Paradise loses, but hey, let's begin!

Serenity's Gentle Touch

In the sun's soft glow, a cat takes a nap,
While birds in the trees flap and flap.
A coconut falls, with a thud and a bounce,
As the beachgoers laugh, they try to denounce.

With a drink made of fruit, all bright and round,
Ice cubes melting fast, they'll soon make a sound.
But hold on tight, for the wind starts to tease,
And here comes a seagull looking for cheese!

Balloons in the air, like puffs of pure joy,
While kids chase the waves, a giggling convoy.
But beware of the splashes, they fly like confetti,
As sunscreen applications are far from ready!

So let the laughter roll with each playful wave,
In these blissful moments, we find what we crave.
With sunshine as witness, we dance on the sand,
In this lighthearted haven, it's perfectly planned.

Hidden Coves of Contemplation

In a cove where the shadows softly play,
A tortoise ambles slowly on its way.
It trips on a shell, oh what a sight,
While crabs do a dance, oh what a fright!

A hammock swings low between two palm trees,
As squirrels steal snacks with the greatest of ease.
A thought just hit me, as I sip on my drink,
Do fish ever ponder? I really must think!

The breeze whispers secrets we can't quite catch,
While beach towels billow like flags in a match.
With a smile on my face, I lay back and sigh,
Wondering if clouds ever wish they could fly.

As laughter rolls in like the waves on the shore,
I ponder on life and its purpose once more.
Just then a seagull steals my last fry,
Well, at least I've got sand for a place to cry!

The Dance of the Dusk

As the sun dips low, painting skies of grace,
A crab dons a cap and struts in its place.
Fish start to jump, looking oh-so-sly,
While a pelican fumbles, oh dear, oh why?

A conch shell orchestra plays a fine tune,
As dolphins join in, beneath the pale moon.
But wait! What's that? A flip-flop flies,
And lands on a beachgoer – what a surprise!

With sand in our hair and smiles on our face,
We giggle and dance, finding our space.
The tides are our partners, in this vibrant waltz,
While shells race the sunset, oh, what a pulse!

The twilight embraces, as laughter adheres,
In this whimsical world, forgetting our fears.
So let us sway here, with moonlight's embrace,
As crabs keep the beat, in this frolicsome place!

Echoes of the Gentle Surf

Waves crash with laughter, a bubbly embrace,
As children dive in, each sporting a face.
With sand in their toes, and shells in their hair,
They race with the tide, nothing else can compare.

A board floats away, it's quite a bold scene,
As a brave little pup gives it a keen glean.
But oh no, it's stuck! In a whirlpool of foam,
As laughter erupts, calling it back home!

The sun starts to settle, hues fiery and bright,
A starfish plays peek-a-boo, just out of sight.
While someone shouts, "Hey! If you hear me out there,
Toss me a snack, I promise to share!"

So let the surf whisper, secrets from deep,
As seagulls all gather, in the twilight they creep.
With giggles and splashes, as the day turns to night,
In our joyous retreat, everything feels right.

Islands of Imagined Peace

On islands where the seagulls sing,
A coconut's my royal bling.
My flip-flops dance with every wave,
A king of sand, so bold and brave.

The sunbathers are quite a sight,
In sun hats that are far too tight.
They sip their drinks, all frothy and sweet,
While I just chase the crabs on feet.

The ocean whispers tales of fun,
Where every fish wishes to run.
I tell a joke to starfish nearby,
They chuckle back with a twinkly eye.

Beneath the palms, I find my place,
In laughter's warm, embracing space.
The tides roll in, but it's all a tease,
For here, I'll nap, with sand as my fleece.

The Jewel of Serenity

A hammock swings between the trees,
With lemonade that drips like bees.
The parrots squawk their silly tunes,
While I just snooze under my moons.

The sun's a hotball in the sky,
It makes me wish I could just fly.
But with every sip, I feel so fine,
Like jellybeans dipped in sunshine.

The breeze comes in with playful flips,
Tickling my nose as I eat chips.
Neighbors argue 'bout the best drink,
But all I need's a wink and a pink.

On this jewel, I'm in a daze,
Counting clouds in a silly haze.
Should I build a sand castle tall?
Or join the fish in a beach ball brawl?

Mellow Evenings and Ocean Breezes

The sun dips low, a golden sphere,
While waves applaud with a gentle cheer.
Mellow evenings, laughter at play,
As crabs host parties just down the bay.

A dolphin dances, all sleek and spry,
I wave to him; he winks, oh my!
The tide's a jester in swirling gowns,
While I wear flip-flops, the funkiest crowns.

Breezes whisper secrets so light,
Like snippets of gossip from day to night.
My friends make sand angels, what a sight!
All this joy, it feels so right.

With marshmallow clouds in the twilight's glow,
We roast our laughs in a perfect row.
S'mores of giggles, jokes we breed,
In this ocean's rhythm, hearts will lead.

Driftwood Dreams

Upon driftwood dreams, I lie and stare,
The sea whispers secrets, if you dare.
A crab in shades, he's quite the dude,
While I drop my sandwich, oh what rudeness!

The waves ebb and flow with frothy laughs,
Echoing giggles from ocean's staffs.
I tip my hat to a passing cloud,
While it rains confetti, oh, how loud!

A coconut rolls by, wanting to chat,
He says he's tired of being a mat.
I share my chips, and we have a feast,
A snack party, oh, to say the least!

In the palm's shade, dreams get so wild,
And every worry's just a forgotten child.
I swirl in bliss, like a kite on the stream,
In a world of driftwood, I live my dream.

Ebb and Flow of Contentment

In a hammock I sway, oh what a delight,
As I sip on my drink with a fruit so bright.
A crab walks by, looking quite dapper,
I can't help but giggle, it's quite the yapper.

The waves dance nearby, a frothy parade,
Whispers of coconuts, shade they've made.
Seagulls squawk jokes, a comedic show,
Who knew nature's laugh would steal the show?

The sun winks at me, a playful spark,
While I try to juggle oranges in the park.
They roll away, but I just can't care,
A lemur laughs too; life's just a circus affair.

Under palm trees, we twirl and play,
With flip-flops flying in a ballet display.
A day full of whimsy, I'll take it all,
The ebb and flow of joy, I hear nature's call.

Still Waters, Warm Breezes

Still waters shimmer, a mirror in place,
As a lizard passes with a goofy grace.
Breezes come tickling, soft as can be,
I think they're just playing a prank on me!

Flip-flops flapping, a dance on the shore,
I trip on my towel and roll like a floor.
A fish pops its head, and I swear it's grinning,
Guess nature's laughing at my swimming beginning!

The sun has a racket with its bright, shiny rays,
Competing with shadows in a game, quite a play.
Pelicans dive, with finesse and flair,
Droplets like diamonds in the fresh ocean air.

When all is too peaceful, and boredom is near,
I challenge my friend to a race, with a cheer.
But he's in a hammock, not ready to flee,
So I dive in the water, and splash with glee!

Embrace of the Escapade

In a whirlwind of escapades, laughs abound,
We tripped over sandcastles that fell to the ground.
With coconuts grinning, they've joined our fest,
We all share secrets; they're going 'nutty' at best!

The tide rolls in with a giggle and hum,
Blowing my hat to a passing old bum.
We both burst out laughing, it's quite a scene,
Two friends on the beach, living life like a dream!

A parrot swoops down, making jokes while we target,
I catch it with crackers, but it quickly departs.
We chase after laughter, a treasure so grand,
In the embrace of delight, it's all simply planned.

Each moment a memory, we capture like light,
Under the sun's glow, everything feels right.
With good vibes around, and fun on the spree,
The heart finds a rhythm, in harmony free!

Paths to Peace

On sandy paths where the sun likes to play,
We wander with laughter, it's a humorous day.
A slip here and there, as we dance through the sun,
Each step a comedy, we both come undone!

Palm trees entice, like giants on stay,
As if they're chuckling, come join the fray!
The breeze carries whispers of jokes from the shore,
I laugh with the gulls; who could ask for more?

Barefoot adventures, where wildflowers grow,
I stop for a moment to answer the show.
Nature's so funny, with all of its charm,
And I'm the star, with no need for alarm.

With coconuts rolling and surfboards in tune,
We dance with the rhythm beneath the bright moon.
Paths to our peace paved in laughs and cheer,
Funny little moments, forever held dear.

Cascades of Comfort

In the shade of a mango tree,
I sip my drink, oh so carefree.
A lizard does a silly jig,
As I laugh and munch on a twig.

A coconut drops with a loud thud,
My friends call it a 'tropical dud'.
With sand between my toes, I grin,
As palm fronds wave and let the fun begin!

While seagulls squawk and steal my fries,
I throw them crumbs, much to their surprise.
The waves crash in a giddy rhyme,
As ocean breezes dance and chime.

Sunset rolls in, painting the sky,
Me and my friends just passing by.
A hammock swings while we sit tight,
Cracking jokes till the stars shine bright.

The Delicate Dance of Palm Fronds

Palm fronds sway in a hula dance,
While I struggle not to spill my glance.
The breeze decides to play a game,
Whipping my hair, oh, what a shame!

A beach ball bounces, off a rude dude,
With sunglasses on, looking quite shrewd.
We laugh as he dives, a comical flop,
His pride takes a hit, but he won't stop.

A crab with swagger scuttles by,
Pinching the world, oh me, oh my!
We cheer him on, "You go, little mate!"
While sipping our drinks, it feels like fate.

When twilight cloaks the shining day,
We share silly tales and laugh away.
The moonlight glows like a disco ball,
As we cherish the absurd in it all.

Cherishing the Quiet Moments

In the stillness of the afternoon,
A moment's peace feels like a boon.
My ice cream melts just a bit too fast,
As I whisper to waves, 'You won't outlast!'

A squirrel steals my thoughts and my snack,
He hops around, never looks back.
Stubbornly I guard my precious treat,
While the little thief quickens his feat.

Clouds float lazily, little puffs of cheer,
Yet here comes a seagull, oh dear, oh dear!
He eyes my sandwich like it's gold,
And makes a dive, so brazen, so bold.

As the sun sinks low, we watch from afar,
And giggle at life; it's a shining star.
These moments we cherish, absurd but bright,
In the hue of twilight, everything feels right.

Serenity in the Salt Air

Salt air tickles, what a delight,
As I try to fly a kite, what a sight!
It flips and flops, a wild tease,
Just like my attempts at balancing ease.

Nearby, a dog starts barking loud,
Chasing a wave while attracting a crowd.
His joy is contagious, tails wag with glee,
As he plops onto sand, covered in debris.

Two kids dig deep, a castle they build,
The tide approaches, their laughter spilled.
A moat appears, quite the surprise,
As water rushes in, they gasp and rise!

In the fading light, we sit and share,
Silly stories float through the air.
Under the stars, we laugh and play,
Life's saltiness sweetens our day.

Basking in Bliss

Under the sun, we fry and gleam,
A flamingo floats on a pool of cream.
The ice cream melts, drips down my chin,
I laugh so hard, I might just spin.

Seagulls squawk, they steal my fries,
They're sneaky birds, oh what a surprise!
I toss them crumbs, they take a dive,
Amid this chaos, I feel alive.

My flip-flops flop like fish on land,
They dance around, they just can't stand.
The waves roll in, soft bubbles burst,
Here in my hammock, I'm blessed, I'm cursed.

So here's to days that make us grinning,
Where sun and laughter keep us spinning.
With salty air and friends so dear,
I live for moments like this each year.

Seaglass and Silhouettes

Among the shells, I search for glass,
A blue one sparkles, oh, what a class!
I hold it high, a trophy found,
"Look at this treasure!" I yell around.

My shadow's dancing on the shore,
Like a clumsy crab, it falls, it soars.
The ocean giggles, waves at play,
It splashes back, "You can't win today!"

With salty toes, I skip and slip,
My ice-cold drink, I bravely sip.
A coconut falls from a tree above,
I scream and run, but it's just a shove.

So we collect the little things,
The joy that every moment brings.
In sunset hues, we laugh and fret,
Seaglass and silhouettes, no regrets.

Calm in the Canopy

Swinging on vines, I feel like Tarzan,
But truth be told, I'm no brave man.
The monkeys laugh as I descend,
For graceful landings, I don't pretend.

The leaves above shade all my plans,
I bring my lunch, but lose my cans.
A raccoon grins, its eyes aglow,
"Is that your snack?" it seems to glow.

The breeze whispers secrets in my ear,
"Your hammock's cozy, don't you fear."
I doze off fast, with dreams so bold,
Of giant fruits, and stories told.

So here I sway, with laughter's sound,
In nature's maze, where fun is found.
With each new sound, I chuckle soft,
In the canopy, I feel aloft.

The Soft Murmurs of the Sea

The ocean's whispers tickle my ear,
"Come play with us, there's nothing to fear!"
I splash around like a clumsy seal,
The dolphins chuckle, "What's your deal?"

A crab in sandals struts on by,
With shades on top, like a cool passersby.
He waves a claw, gives me a wink,
It's a beach party, we share a drink!

The tides all giggle in their own way,
As kids build castles, then watch them sway.
The sea foam dances, it leaps and twirls,
In this goofy world, every joy unfurls.

So let's embrace this playful spree,
With sandy toes and hearts so free.
Each wave's a joke, a laugh, a cheer,
The beach is life, come hold it near!